KIDNEY DISEASE COOI

25 easy and delicious recipes to manage and reverse renal disease

Dr. Malvin Harison

TABLE OF CONTENT

25. Vegetable and Tofu Stir-Fry

INTRODUCTION

Is it possible to eat vegetarian renal food? Yes! Recommended and possible! For those who adhere to a renal/kidney diet, this book provides examples of low-sodium vegetarian meal ideas.

For individuals with renal illness, integrating vegan dinners into your eating routine isn't just possible, yet additionally solid! Meals that are vegetarian assist in slowing the kidney's progression. Recent studies have shown that dialysis patients can get a lot of protein without meat and sometimes have better or equal phos control (even with some extra beans!)

Dietitians have gathered 25 meatless recipes for you to integrate into your kidney diet. Talk to your dietitian about ways to supplement meatless meals to meet your daily protein goal if you are on dialysis and need more protein. This book is a great resource for you.

Benefits of eating a plant based diet for kidney health

Eating a plant-based diet can have numerous benefits for renal health. The kidneys are responsible for filtering waste and excess fluids from the blood, so it's important to keep them functioning properly. Here are some of the benefits of a plant-based diet for renal health:

Lowering blood pressure: High blood pressure is a leading cause of kidney disease. Plant-based diets, especially those that are low in sodium, have been shown to lower blood pressure and reduce the risk of kidney disease.

Reducing inflammation: Chronic inflammation can damage the kidneys over time. Plant-based diets are rich in anti-inflammatory foods such as fruits, vegetables, and whole grains, which can help reduce inflammation in the body and protect the kidneys.

Improving glucose control: Diabetes is a leading cause of kidney disease. Plant-based diets can improve glucose control and reduce the risk of developing diabetes, which in turn can help protect the kidneys.

Lowering cholesterol: High cholesterol levels can contribute to kidney disease. Plant-based diets have been shown to lower cholesterol levels and reduce the risk of kidney disease.

Increasing fiber intake: Plant-based diets are typically high in fiber, which can help promote regular bowel movements and prevent constipation. This can be particularly important for people with kidney disease, who may experience digestive issues.

Reducing the workload on the kidneys: Animal protein can be hard on the kidneys, as they have to work harder to filter the waste products produced during protein metabolism. Plant-based diets are typically lower in protein and can reduce the workload on the kidneys.

25 delicious and nutritious kidney friendly recipes

1. Armando's Chiles Rellenos:

Ingredients: 4 ounces cream cheese; 1/4 cup sliced fresh mushrooms; 1 tablespoon carrot; 1 teaspoon onion; 2 California green chili peppers; 1 egg white; 1 teaspoon all-purpose white flour; 1 cup canola oil.

Instructions:

Step 1: To make stuffing, combine cream cheese, mushrooms, carrots, and onion in a bowl. Put away in the cooler until bean stew peppers are ready.

Step 2: A medium-sized frying pan should be used. Place peppers in a container and meal, turning a few times, until the skin bubbles. Take off the heat. Peel the skin off the peppers when they are cool enough to handle.

Step 3: Open chili peppers along their length and gently stuff half of the cream cheese mixture inside each one.

Step 4: Beat the egg whites and flour in a separate bowl until stiff. Use the egg mixture to coat each stuffed chili pepper.

Step 5: In a saucepan, add enough canola oil to cover the pan by about an inch. Set the heat to medium-high.

step 6: Cautiously place bean stew peppers in the hot oil and sear until brilliant brown, turning once. Serve warm.

2. Breakfast Burrito

Ingredients: 4 eggs, 3 tablespoons Ortega green chiles, diced, 1/4 teaspoon ground cumin, 1/2 teaspoon hot pepper sauce, 2 flour tortillas, burrito-size

Instructions:
Step 1: A medium skillet should be sprayed with nonstick cooking spray and heated over low heat.

Step 2: In a bowl, beat eggs with green chiles, cumin, and hot sauce.

Empty eggs into a skillet and cook and mix for 1 to 2 minutes until eggs are finished.

Step 3: The tortillas can be heated in a separate skillet over medium heat or in the microwave for 20 seconds. Roll each tortilla into a burrito shape and cover it with half of the egg mixture.

3. Crunchy Tofu Stir Fry

Ingredients: 16 ounces extra firm tofu, 1/2 red bell pepper, 1 garlic clove, 1 tablespoon reduced-sodium soy sauce, 1 tablespoon lime juice, 2 teaspoons sugar, 2 tablespoons cornstarch, 2 egg whites, one cup of unseasoned bread crumbs, one tablespoon of canola oil, one tablespoon of sesame oil, one cup fresh broccoli florets, 1 teaspoon of herb seasoning blend, 1/8 teaspoon of black pepper, 1/8 teaspoon of cayenne pepper, 1/2 teaspoon of sesame seeds, 2 cups of steamed white rice.

Instructions:
Step 1: Chop the clove of garlic and slice the bell pepper in strips.
In a small bowl, combine sugar, lime juice, and reduced-sodium soy sauce, Place aside.

Step 2: In three separate dishes, put cornstarch, egg whites, and bread scraps. To coat tofu cubes, first coat them in bread crumbs and then in egg whites.

Step 3: Stir-fry-coated tofu in canola oil in a skillet or wok until crispy and golden brown. Set the tofu aside from the pan.

Step 4: Add sesame oil to the same pan. and warm it. Broccoli and red bell pepper strips are stir-fried until crisp and tender. Cook for one minute before adding chopped garlic, Mrs. Dash seasoning, black pepper, and cayenne pepper.

Step 5: Toss the vegetables and tofu back into the pan. Sprinkle the sesame seeds on top and stir in the mixture of soy and lime juice. Divide into four portions and remove from the heat. With 1/2 cup of rice, serve.

4. Garlicky Penne Pasta with Asparagus:

Ingredients: 2 tablespoons butter, 2 tablespoons olive oil, 6 cloves garlic, 1/8 teaspoon red pepper flakes, 1 pound asparagus, 1/4 teaspoon hot sauce, 2 teaspoons lemon juice, 1/2 teaspoon black pepper, 8 ounces uncooked whole wheat penne pasta, and 1/4 cup shredded Parmesan cheese.

Instructions:

Step 1: Asparagus can be cut into 2" pieces. Grate garlic.

Step 2: Olive oil and butter should be heated in a medium skillet over medium heat. Sauté the red pepper flakes and garlic for two to three minutes.

Step 3: In a skillet, cook the asparagus, Tabasco sauce, lemon juice, and black pepper for 6 minutes until crisp and tender.

Step 4: Transfer the drained pasta to a bowl. Add asparagus and throw.
Serve with cheese shredded on top.

5. Omelet with Summer Vegetable

Ingredients: nonstick cooking spray 1/4 cup thawed frozen whole kernel corn; 1/3 cup chopped zucchini; 3 tablespoons chopped green onion; 2 tablespoons water; 1/4 teaspoon Extra Spicy herb seasoning blend; 2 large egg whites; 1 large egg; 1 ounce shredded low-fat sharp cheddar cheese.

Instructions:

Step 1: Cover the dish with a cooking shower. In a pan, add the zucchini, corn, and onions; 4 minutes, or until the vegetables are crisp-tender, sauté them. Take off the heat.

Step 2: In a nonstick 10-inch skillet, heat the oil to medium-high. Using a whisk, thoroughly combine the water, pepper, egg whites, and egg in a bowl.

Step 3: Cover the container with a cooking shower. In a pan, pour the egg mixture; cook for about 2 minutes or until the edges begin to set.

Step 4: A spatula should be used to lift the edges of the omelet gently and tilt the pan so that the uncooked egg mixture touches the pan.

Step 5: Spoon the vegetable combination onto half of the omelet, and sprinkle cheddar over the vegetable blend. Relax the omelet with a spatula and overlap it into equal parts. It should be Cooked for an extra two minutes or until the cheese is melted. Place the omelet on a plate with care.

6. Pasta Primavera

Ingredients: 12 ounces of uncooked pasta; 12 ounces of frozen mixed vegetables; 14 ounces low-sodium chicken broth; two tablespoons of all-purpose white flour; 1/4 cup half-and-half creamer; 1/4 teaspoon garlic powder; 1/4 cup grated Parmesan cheese.

Instructions:

Step 1: Cook the pasta and vegetables separately, omitting the salt. Drain.

Step 2: Pour low-sodium chicken stock into a medium-sized stockpot and intensity on low intensity.

Step 3: Whisk vigorously as you add the flour to the broth to prevent clumps from forming.
Stir in the half-and-half and garlic powder.

Step 4: The mixture should slightly thicken after 5 to 10 minutes of simmering on low heat.
While simmering, stirring occasionally.
Include pasta and cooked vegetables. Cook until thoroughly heated.
Serve with Parmesan cheese sprinkled on top.

7. Tempeh Pita Sandwiches

Ingredients: 8 ounces of tempeh, 2 tablespoons sesame oil, 2 tablespoons balsamic vinegar, 1 small onion, 1 red bell pepper, 1/2 cup mushrooms, 2 pieces 6-inch pita bread, 4 teaspoons mayonnaise

Instructions:
Step 1: Slice tempeh into 12 slices. Slice the mushrooms, bell pepper, and onion very thinly.
Step 2: Heat 1 tablespoon of the sesame oil in a large skillet over medium heat. Cook each side of the sliced tempeh until browned for 3 to 4 minutes. Cook for one minute after adding the

balsamic vinegar; Cook for an additional minute on the flip side. Take tempeh out of the skillet.

Step 3: Add the remaining sesame oil to the skillet and intensity over medium intensity. Cook until the mushrooms, onion, and bell pepper are tender.

Step 4: Open the pita in half to create a pocket. Spread one teaspoon of mayonnaise over each half. Each pita half should have three tempeh pieces and a quarter of the vegetable mixture. Serve right away.

8. Vegetarian Egg Fried Rice:

Ingredients: 2 cloves of garlic, 1 tablespoon fresh ginger root, 1 cup fresh carrots, 1 cup yellow onion, 1 cup extra firm tofu, 1/2 cup cilantro, 1/2 cup green onions, 6 large eggs, 1 tablespoon reduced-sodium soy sauce, 3 tablespoons canola oil, 1/2 cup green peas, 1/4 teaspoon dry mustard, and 4 cups cooked rice.

Instructions:

Step1: Slice carrots. Dice yellow onion and tofu. Chop the green onions and cilantro.

Make an omelet by beating eggs and sautéing them in a pan. Slash cooked eggs into pieces and put them away.

Step 2: The oil should be heated in a skillet over low heat. Tofu, peas, dry mustard, ginger, carrots, yellow onion, and stirred in.

Step 3: Add rice, eggs chopped, and soy sauce when the carrots have softened. Mix and remove from heat.
Mix in cilantro and green onions.

9. Triple Berry Salad with Cottage Cheese:

Ingredients: 2 cups fresh strawberries; 1 cup fresh blackberries; 1 cup fresh blueberries; 1/4 cup lemon juice; 2 cups low-fat cottage cheese; 1/8 teaspoon cinnamon.

Instructions:
Step 1: Thoroughly wash all berries.

Step 2: Combine the remaining berries in a bowl with the sliced strawberries.
Juice some lemons.

Step 3: Place berries on top of the cottage cheese on a serving plate or bowl.
Sprinkle with ground cinnamon (discretionary).

10. Vegetable Dish Delite

Ingredients
1 teaspoon olive oil
1/2 cup yellow summer squash
1/2 cup low-sodium canned green beans
8 ounces All Whites liquid egg whites
1/8 teaspoon dark pepper
1 scramble paprika

Instructions:
Microwave arrangement:
Step 1: Oil the lower part of a microwave dish with olive oil.

Step 2: Squash and green beans should be sliced thinly around the dish's edge.
Add the egg replacer.

Step 3: Paprika and pepper are used to season it. Cover and cook on high for 4 to 4 and a half minutes, turning once.

How to prepare a stovetop:
In a frying pan, heat olive oil.
Daintily sauté squash.
Add green beans to the container.
Sprinkle it with pepper and paprika, then add the egg substitute.
Cook over medium heat, covered, until the center is firm.
Partition fifty and serve hot.

11. Vegan Pizza

Ingredients:
1/2 cup red onion
1/2 cup green ringer pepper
1/2 cup mushroom pieces
1/2 cup pineapple goodies
1/2 cup part-skim destroyed mozzarella cheddar
2 tablespoons ground Parmesan cheddar
1 cup Simmered Red Pepper Pureed tomatoes
Simple Pizza Mixture
Instructions:
Step 1: Dice the onion; Slice the bell pepper.

Get ready for Simple Pizza Batter and Red Pepper Pureed Tomato recipes.

Step 2: Shape the pizza dough into two flat 12" pizza crusts and heat the oven to 425 degrees Fahrenheit.

Step 3: Each pizza should have 1/2 cup of Roasted Red Pepper Tomato Sauce on top.

Step 4: Add pineapple, mushrooms, red onion, and bell pepper to the top.
Sprinkle mozzarella and Parmesan cheese on top.

Step 5: Heat for 12 to 16 minutes until effervescent and sautéed.

12. Veggie Strata

Ingredients: 7 slices of sourdough bread, 1/2" thick; 1 cup onion; 1 cup raw mushrooms; 1 cup red bell pepper; 1 tablespoon unsalted butter; 15 fresh spinach leaves; 7 large eggs; 3/4 cup half-and-half creamer; 1 teaspoon Worcestershire sauce; 1 teaspoon hot sauce;

1/2 teaspoon black pepper; 1 ounce shredded sharp cheddar cheese, ¼ cup tarragon vinegar.

Instructions

Step 1: Bake the bread after cutting it into cubes for 15 minutes at 225° F on a baking sheet. After turning the cubes over, bake for another 15 minutes, or until crisp and dry.

Step 2: Dice onion, mushrooms, and ringer pepper.

Step 3: In a small skillet, sauté the onion, mushrooms, and red pepper in butter.
Oil a 9" square baking dish with a nonstick cooking splash. Orchestrate half of the bread 3D squares in a solitary layer in the dish and sprinkle with half of the vegetable combination. Organize spinach leaves on top.

Step 4: Structure a second layer with residual bread and vegetables on top.

Step 5: Whisk together the eggs, vinegar, Worcestershire sauce, hot sauce, black pepper, and half-and-half creamer. Sprinkle evenly over the bread.

Step 6: Refrigerate the surface for at least one hour or overnight with plastic wrap.

For twenty minutes, let strata stand at room temperature.

Step 7: Remove the plastic wrap and bake for 50 minutes at 325 degrees Fahrenheit.

Sprinkle cheddar cheese on top after removing the pan from the oven. Cook for an extra 10 minutes or until a blade embedded close to the middle confesses all.

Cut into 9 servings and serve hot.

13. Tofu and Veggie Frittata

Ingredients: 350 grams of firm tofu that has been drained; 3/4 grams aquafaba made from cooked or canned chickpeas; 1/4 cup plus 2 tablespoons chickpea flour or all-purpose flour; 1 medium potato that has been diced (1 cup); 1 medium red bell pepper that has been diced (1 cup); 1 large zucchini that has been diced (2 cups); 4 green onions that have been sliced (1 cup); ½ cup finely chopped cilantro; 2 tbsp yeast,1.5 tbsp of miso, 1 tbsp of garlic powder,

1 tbsp of onion powder, ¼ tsp of turmeric, ¼ tsp of sea salt, 1 tsp of red pepper flakes (adjust as needed)

Instructions:

Step 1: Blend the tofu, aquafaba (liquid from canned or cooked chickpea), flour, nutritional yeast, miso, turmeric, sea salt, and red pepper flakes in a blender to make a smooth batter.

Cut the potato, zucchini, and red bell pepper into small pieces. Finely hack green onions and cilantro.

Step 2: Add diced chime pepper and potatoes to a dish and sauté for around 10 minutes, until the potatoes are cooked.

Mix in the cilantro, green onions, and zucchini. In about 5 minutes, sauté the vegetables until tender.

Step 3: Place the cooked vegetables in a pie dish that is 8 inches across. Mix thoroughly after pouring the batter over the vegetables.

Step 4: The frittata should brown on top after 60 minutes of baking. Allow it to cool for a few minutes after removing it from the oven. Serve with slicing. Enjoy!

14. Roasted Red Bell Pepper Cauliflower Pizza:

Ingredients:

Half of cauliflower head with the stalk removed; quarter cup of grated parmesan; one tbsp of turmeric; one tbsp of Italian seasoning; quarter tbsp of salt; one egg; half cup of shredded mozzarella cheese; two red bell peppers; one tbsp of olive oil; one teaspoon for drizzling on peppers and garlic; 2-3 cloves of garlic with the peel; 5 sprigs of fresh basil; one tbsp of corn-starch (or potato starch).

Instructions

Step 1: The oven should be heated to 450 degrees F.

Step 2: Place the unpeeled garlic cloves and cleaned bell peppers on a baking sheet to prevent the garlic from burning.

Step 3: Sprinkle on 1 tsp of oil and a smidgen of salt and heat for 30 minutes until the red chime peppers look delicate and brown.

Step 4: Remove the cauliflower from the food processor and pulse it until it is crumbly and has the consistency of rice. Do this while the peppers are baking.

Step 5: Spread the riced cauliflower out in a single layer on a baking sheet that has been lined with parchment paper, and bake for 15 minutes in the same oven as the bell peppers and garlic.

Step 6: Verify the garlic and red bell peppers. When it's ready, take it out of the oven and let it cool for ten minutes.

Step 7: Strip and trim the stem off of the peppers and strip the garlic.

Step 8: Combine garlic, peppers, olive oil and corn starch in a food processor at a very high speed until it becomes smooth.

Step 9: In a little pot, mix the ringer pepper sauce for 10-15 minutes on low intensity until the sauce thickens and puts away.

Step 10: Remove the riced cauliflower from the oven and place it on a clean cheese towel or dish towel once it has cooled.

Step 11: Remove the water and any excess moisture by squeezing it out.

Step 12: Add the riced cauliflower, spices, parmesan, salt, and egg to a large bowl. Blend well.

Step 13: On a baking sheet that has been lined with parchment paper, press the dough into a circle that is 1/4 inch thick.

Step 14: At 400°F, bake for 30 minutes until golden. Bake the crust on the other side for an additional ten minutes.

Step 15: Remove it from the stove and add the simmered red pepper sauce, mozzarella, and basil. In this video, learn how to chiffonade basil leaves.

Step 16: Bake for another 5 to 10 minutes, or until the cheese is melted.

Enough for two small pizzas! Enjoy the slice!

15. Warm Falafel Wraps:

Ingredients:

400 grams of low-sodium chickpeas that have been rinsed and drained (as dry as possible) 1/4 red onion, roughly chopped, 1/2 cloves of garlic, roughly chopped, 10 grams of flat-leaf or curly parsley, roughly chopped, 1 teaspoon ground cumin, 1 teaspoon ground coriander, ½ teaspoon ground harissa, or chili powder, 2 tablespoons all-purpose flour, 2 tablespoons olive oil, 1 tablespoon of tahini, 2 teaspoons of mayonnaise, 1 tbsp of milk and lemon juice, 2 pita bread.

Extra optional garnish

Cucumber finely sliced in 1/4 cup, shredded lettuce in 1/4 cup, and red onion finely sliced in 1/4 cup.

Instructions:

Step 1: Channel the chickpeas and wipe them off with kitchen paper. Place the onion, two garlic cloves, parsley, cumin, coriander, harissa paste, tahini, flour, and a little salt in a food processor. To combine, pulse. Smooth pureeing is not recommended. With your hands, form four patties.

Step 2: In a nonstick frying pan, heat the oil and fry the burgers for three minutes on each side until they are lightly golden.

Step 3: Prepare the garlic aioli while the patties are cooking. Make a smooth, creamy sauce by combining the remaining garlic cloves, which have been finely chopped, with the mayonnaise, milk, and lemon juice.
To make a more durable pocket, divide the pita bread in half and lightly trim one half so that it fits inside the other.

Step 4: Stuff two patties into the half-cut pita bread after the patties have finished cooking. Add shredded lettuce, sliced cucumber, and sliced red onion on top. Serve with the aioli drizzled on top!

Note: This recipe has a lot of fiber but also a lot of carbohydrates. If you are a diabetic and have to deal with your carb consumption, we recommend utilizing just 50% of one pita, as opposed to multiplying them as Gourmet expert

Kris proposes. For a lower-carb option, these patties would also be delicious served with a salad.

16. Prepared Eggs with Basil Pesto

Ingredients:
2 Eggs, huge
½ tsp Olive Oil
1-50g bundle Basil, new (kale is another sound and delectable choice if basil is inaccessible)
2 Tbsp Parmesan cheddar, ground
½ tsp Sunflower seeds, unsalted
½ tsp Lemon juice
½ Lemon zing
2 Tbsp Chime peppers, red, diced
2 Tbsp Zucchini, diced
2 Tbsp Onions, Spanish, diced
¼ tsp Cayenne Pepper
½ tsp Garlic, new

Instructions
Step 1: Splash baking dish with cooking shower.

Step 2: Add eggs to the dish. On top, add vegetables.

Step 3: Sprinkle on some cayenne pepper.
It should be baked for about 10-15 minutes at 375 degrees F.

Step 4: Make pesto in the meantime: In a food processor, blend basil, olive oil, parmesan, sunflower, lemon juice, and lemon zest until a purée forms.
At the point when prepared eggs are out of the broiler, place a dab of pesto in the middle.
Enjoy!

Expert's Tips:
To cut down on prep time, vegetables can be cut a day in advance.
The basil pesto can be pureed the day before and stored for three days in the refrigerator.
Basil can also be substituted for kale.
Rather than cayenne pepper, stew powder, or curry powder can be utilized.

17. Plant-based Bean Bourguignon

Ingredients:
1 can (425g) Dark Beans, canned, no salt added, depleted

1/2 cup slashed new mushrooms

4 Medium onions, Spanish, diced

¼ Cup Cannellini Beans depleted

1/3 cup red wine (discretionary), or water for deglazing

3 cups Vegetable stock, no salt added

1 Carrots, medium diced

20g Parsley, generally slashed

1 Tbsp Garlic, new, minced

½ tsp Dark pepper

1 Tbsp Olive oil

1 tsp Smoked paprika

4 Tbsp Flour, universally handy

3 branches Thyme, new

Instructions:

Step 1: Add oil to the pot, or Dutch broiler and sauté mushrooms with smoked paprika. Set aside the mushrooms and any liquids.

Step 2: Cook the onions in the pan until they are lightly browned. Add the garlic and carrots and lightly sauté.

Step 3: Add the flour, pepper, and thyme.
If wine is used, use water or wine to deglaze the pan.

Step 4: Turn the heat up to medium-high and stir until the mixture becomes thick. Heat up less. Scratch the base while mixing to eliminate every one of the pieces on the lower part of the pot.

Step 5: Include the beans, Cook the carrots over medium heat. About twenty to thirty minutes. The pot should be kept covered while it becomes steam.
After 5 minutes, add the mushrooms and any liquid that was left over.
Sprinkle Parsley on top.
Enjoy!

Chef's Advice:
To enhance the flavors of this classic French stew, add a lot of aromatics like rosemary and thyme.
Making your own is a better way to ensure that your stock or broth does not contain sodium if you are feeling brave. By adding fluid to a hot

container, all of the food buildups will lift, giving your dish added flavor.

For additional flavor, red wine can be added in place of water. The flavor will be the only thing that remains because the alcohol will cook.

While adding the thyme, stand for ten minutes or something like that, and you can select the stems and the leaves will stay in the stew.

18. Vegetable Chili:

Ingredients

1/2 diced onions, 2 stalks of celery, 1 bell pepper, 1 carrot, 1 tablespoon of diced celery, 1 tablespoon of diced carrot, 1 tablespoon of diced bell pepper, 1 tablespoon of chili powder, 2 teaspoons of dried oregano, 1 tablespoon of chili powder, 425 grams of kidney beans, 425 grams of garbanzo beans,

425 grams of black beans, 1 tablespoon of olive oil, 14 ounces of low-sodium vegetable

Instructions

Step 1: Combine all ingredients in your slow cooker pot, and cook for 4 hours on high heat, or 8 hours on low heat.

19. Sweet Crustless Quiche

Ingredients: 3 large eggs, 1/2 cup flour, 250 grams, 250 milliliters of 2% milk.

sweet filling:

¼ cup butter, 2 teaspoons brown sugar, 3 small apples diced.

Instructions:

Step 1: In a bowl, crack eggs and whisk in each ingredient, dairy, then flour, until most of the lumps are smoothed out. Add three medium apples, sliced or diced. Spices and salt, if any, should be added.

Note: You could heat and serve this combination all alone.

Step 2: Cook the filling ingredients in a skillet over medium heat until heated through and bubbling, about 15-20 minutes.

Step 3: Cover a deep-dish pie pan or an 88-inch cake pan thoroughly with cooking spray to prevent the quiche from sticking. Pour the cooked documenting (2-3 cups) into the lubed baking skillet and spread daintily to uniformly convey. Bake at 350 degrees for 40 to 45 minutes, or until a knife comes out clean and the top is golden brown, then top with the crustless quiche mixture.

20. Savory Crustless Quiche

Ingredients:

3 big eggs

1 cup 2% milk (250 ml)

1/2 cup flour (125 g)

Appetizing Filling:

3 slices diced of bacon

1 cup of onions, diced (250 g)

1 cup of mushrooms, diced (250 g)

2/3 cup of green beans, canned, unsalted (100g) pinch of salt, pepper and any other spices are optional.

Instructions:

Step 1: In a bowl, crack eggs and whisk in each ingredient, dairy, then flour, until most of the lumps are smoothed out. Add 3 slices of bacon sliced into dice, 250 grams of diced onions, 250 grams of diced mushrooms, and 1/3 cup canned, unsalted green beans, 100 grams. Spices and salt, if any, should be added.

Note: You could heat and serve this combination all alone.

Step 2: In a skillet on medium intensity, cook the filling fixings until warmed through and foaming - roughly 15-20 minutes.

Note: Hold the green beans and add them at the finish to keep them from getting soft.

Step 3: Cover a deep-dish pie pan or an 88-inch cake pan thoroughly with cooking spray to prevent the quiche from sticking. Pour the cooked documenting (2-3 cups) into the lubed baking skillet and spread daintily to uniformly convey. Bake at 350 degrees for 40 to 45 minutes, or until a knife comes out clean and the top is golden brown, then top with the crustless quiche mixture.

21. Red Lentil Dahl

Ingredients:

1 cup red lentils, ready as portrayed to diminish potassium content

1 T canola oil

1/2 tsp cumin seeds

1 (2-inch cinnamon stick) or 1 tsp

1 cup diced yellow onion

1 green stew pepper, stemmed, cultivated, and minced (serrano for fiery, jalapeno for milder)
4 garlic cloves, minced
1 T finely minced ginger root
1/2 tsp ground turmeric
1/2 tsp ground cardamom
1/2 tsp paprika
1/4 tsp fit salt (or overlook to additionally diminish sodium)
1 medium tomato, diced
Juice one portion of a lemon
slashed cilantro leaves to decorate

Instructions:

To set up the lentils:

Step 1: Put the lentils in a bowl of water for at least 12 hours—do this before going to bed!

Then, dispose of the dowsing water (presently loaded with potassium), and flush the vegetables

Step 2: Place the flushed lentils in a medium pan alongside 3 cups of room-temperature water. Lentils should cook for 20 minutes if the heat is set to medium.

To get the seasonings ready:
Step 1: The oil should be heated in a small skillet over low heat. Add the cinnamon stick or powder and cumin seeds; cook until fragrant for 60 to 90 seconds.

Step 2: Include the ginger, garlic, green chili, and onion; cook the onions until they become translucent, about 4 to 6 minutes.

Step 3: To the pan, add the tomato, turmeric, cardamom, paprika, salt, and pepper.
In about two to three minutes, cook the tomato until it starts to break apart. If you use a cinnamon stick, throw it away.

Step 4; After the lentils have finished cooking, remove any excess water and add the spiced onion mixture to the lentils. Stir in the juice of the lemon.

Step 5: Chop some cilantro on top; accompany with basmati rice.

22. Broiled Spaghetti Squash With Kale and Parm

Ingredients:
1 huge spaghetti squash
2 Tbsp + 1 tsp extra-virgin olive oil
2 tsp oregano leaves
2 garlic cloves, minced
½ tsp red stew drops
1 huge bundle of kale
½ cup Parmesan cheddar, finely ground

Instructions:
Step 1: Preheat the stove to 350°F.
Part the spaghetti squash in half longwise. Scrape the seeds out with a large spoon before throwing them away.

Step 2: Drizzle two tablespoons of olive oil over the cut side of the spaghetti squash before placing it on a baking sheet with a rim. Garlic, oregano, and chili flakes are some of the toppings. Turn them over so they are chopped side down (this will empower them to cook quicker). In about 45 minutes, bake the squash in the middle of the oven until the flesh is fork-tender. Put away to cool somewhat, around 5 minutes. Scoop the fibers from the squash halves with a large spoon and fork and place them in a large bowl. Throw delicately to isolate the strands so they look like spaghetti.

Step 3: In the meantime, wash the kale and eliminate and dispose of the stems. Tear the leaves into large pieces about the size of a small bite. Utilizing a salad spinner, completely dry.

Step 4: The kale should go into a big bowl. The remaining 1 teaspoon of olive oil should only be used to lightly coat the leaves. Roast the leaves for 12 to 14 minutes, or until crisp and bright green, on two baking sheets with rims. Put away.

Step 5: To assemble, layer the crispy kale chips on top of the spaghetti squash on a large platter. Sprinkle with parmesan and salt and pepper, to taste.

23. Eggplant & Chickpea Curry:

Ingredients: 2 small eggplants or aubergines; 2 tablespoons sunflower oil; 1 tablespoon brown or black mustard seeds; 10 to 12 curry leaves; 2 finely chopped onions; 2 dried chilies; 4 teaspoons garam masala; 2 teaspoons ground coriander; 2 teaspoons turmeric; 200 milliliters low-fat yogurt and vegetable broth, 3 tomatoes that have been quartered; 540 milliliters canned chickpeas that have been rinsed

Instructions:

Step 1: Half of the eggplants should be browned on each side for 2-3 minutes in a large pan, preferably nonstick, until golden brown and crisp on all sides. Scoop onto a plate, then repeat with additional oil and the remaining eggplants before putting everything away. If you don't have a non-stick pan, coat the eggplant with oil and roast it for 15-20 minutes in an oven heated to 400 degrees until browned.

Step 2: Curry leaves and the remaining oil should be added to the pan with the mustard seeds. Fry for 30 seconds to release the aroma. Continue to cook, stirring in the onions, until they begin to brown and become soft. Fry for an additional minute, then stir in the spices and dried chilies with a spoonful of the thick yogurt. Tomatoes, vegetable broth, and the remaining yogurt should be added. Simmer until thick and saucy, 25 to 30 minutes.

Step 3: Add the eggplant and chickpeas and stir. Keep simmering for about 5 minutes, or until the eggplants are tender and everything is hot.
Serve with warm naan bread or rice, sprinkled with a few extra curry leaves, and fried in a little oil if you like.

24. Tofu Fingers

Ingredients:
1 tsp tamari sauce
2 tbsp water
½ cup cornflake scraps
1 tsp preparation (garlic powder, curry, paprika, or other zest)
1 ½ cups (12 oz) firm tofu

Instructions

Step 1: Join the tamari and water in a little bowl.

Step 2: In another bowl, combine as one the cornflake morsels and prepare.

Step 3: The tofu should be dipped in the tamari first, then the seasoning mixture.

Step 4: Wipe the tofu slices lightly with vegetable oil before placing them on a baking sheet.

Step 5: Bake for 20 minutes at 350 degrees Fahrenheit, turning once to brown on both sides.

25. Vegetable and Tofu Stir-Fry

Ingredients:

1 cup long grain rice 2 and 1/2 tbsp hoisin sauce 2 tbsp fresh lime juice 454 grams medium firm tofu prepared with calcium sulfate, cut into 1/2-inch cubes 1 tbsp canola oil 1 carrot, cut into thin strips 1 bell pepper, cut into thin strips 1 tbsp grated fresh ginger, 2 cups bean sprouts 4

scallions, cut into thin, 2 tbsp roasted peanuts, quarter cup of cilantro.

Instructions:
Step 1: Whisk together the hoisin sauce with lime juice.

Step 2: In a large skillet, heat the oil to medium-high heat. Cook, stirring, for two minutes before adding the ginger, bell pepper, and carrot. Include the bean sprouts and tofu.

Step 3: Cook, stirring frequently, for 3 to 4 minutes or until the vegetables are slightly tender. The bean sprouts must be fully cooked to ensure food safety.

Step 4: Serve the vegetables over rice by tossing them with the hoisin sauce mixture.
If desired, sprinkle with the peanuts, cilantro, and scallions.
Take note that some hoisin sauces contain potassium as a preservative; look for one that does not!

Made in the USA
Monee, IL
17 August 2023

41176893R00026